*Indulge yourself
and your guests with a
traditional English Pudding.*

# The
# ETIQUETTE
## of
# ENGLISH
# PUDDINGS

*Copper Beech Publishing*

This edition published in Great Britain by
Copper Beech Publishing Ltd
© Copper Beech Publishing Ltd 1996

ISBN 1 898617 12-0

A CIP catalogue record for this book is available from the British
Library.

Editor: Julie Lessels
Cover Design: Geoff Gillard

*Copper Beech Gift Books*
Copper Beech Publishing Ltd
P O Box 159 East Grinstead
Sussex England RH19 4FS

**"Life's a pudding full of plums"**

Sir W S Gilbert 1836–1911

*Are you missing a good old-fashioned pudding?*

*In Victorian times, long slow cooking like steaming was very popular. Puddings could be left to steam in a pot of water on the kitchen fire or stove, and the water could be 'topped up' until the pudding was ready for the table.*

*Boiled puddings were generally shortened or made light with suet, although butter may be used in its place. The pudding will be lighter if boiled in a cloth, but easier to keep in shape if boiled in a basin. Puddings were, of course a way of sweetening the palate as well as filling up.*

*Puddings have been enjoyed for centuries, and Queen Victoria and Prince Albert, had puddings named after them.*

*The railways were one of the big successes of the nineteenth century, offering ordinary people a method of transport which was safer and speedier than ever before, and soon the railways too were celebrated - with Railway Pudding!*

*These Victorian recipes also considered those who could not afford much in the way of ingredients, so you will find Half Pay Pudding, Economical Fritters and ways of using fruits found by the wayside like Summer Pudding, the recipe for which has hardly changed in 100 years.*

*Enjoy these traditional English puddings and etiquette notes.*

# Puddings

## Dark Treacle Pudding

Take a quarter of a pound of very finely chopped suet, six ounces of dark treacle, a quarter of a pound of flour, two ounces of fine bread crumbs, one tablespoonful of moist sugar, one egg, and three table spoonfuls of milk. Beat the egg well, then mix it with the milk, and afterwards with the other ingredients. Put into a buttered mould, and boil three hours. To be served with wine or brandy sauce.

### Recipe
*for Wine or Brandy Sauce*

*Make a custard with half a pint milk, quarter of a pint of cream, the yolks of four eggs well beaten, sugar to taste, and a small glassful of wine or brandy. Place in a saucepan of boiling water, keep on stirring one way. As soon as your custard becomes hot and begins to thicken, instantly take it off the fire or it will begin to curdle and keep stirring till it cools.*

*Please note: do not add the brandy till you take it off the fire.*

## Railway Pudding

Mix well one tea cupful flour, one tea cupful sugar, half tea cupful milk, one ounce butter, one egg, one teaspoonful baking powder and put into buttered tin, bake twenty minutes in quick oven, cut in half, spread with jam, sprinkle sugar over.

## Ravensworth Pudding

Take three large apples, and then pulp them; take one pint of cream, two handfuls of fine bread crumbs, half a pound of pounded loaf sugar, the grated rind of two lemons and six eggs, using only the yolks of four. Mix all well together, beating the eggs thoroughly, the yolks first and then the whites. Well butter a pudding mould, throw in a handful of fine bread crumbs, toss them round so that they may stick to the butter all round the mould, and shake out any that are loose, then pour in the above mixture and bake an hour and a half.

Serve immediately it is ready with a sauce of butter melted with arrowroot, and a glass of rum or brandy!

## St Leonard's Custard Pudding

Put one tablespoonful of flour into a stewpan with two ounces of butter, and stir over a gentle fire till quite smooth, adding by degrees half a pint of milk and two ounces of sugar rubbed on lemon; stir all together over the fire till it becomes thick, but do not let it boil; turn into a basin and when nearly cold, add the yolks of three eggs. Line your dish with puff paste, then spread a layer of any kind of jam on the paste at the bottom of the dish, pour the custard on the jam, and bake one hour. Whip the whites of the three eggs quite stiff, with two tablespoonfuls of powdered sugar, and put on the top ten minutes before you send to table. The pudding should then be returned to the oven after the eggs are placed on the top, just to set them, and give the top a slight brown colour.

## Hanover Pudding

Grate finely the crumb of a roll, and mince as fine as possible the rind of a lemon, add a quarter of a pound of fine sugar and of fresh butter, the juice of half a lemon, and the yolks of four eggs well beaten, and the whites of two. Set the whole on the fire in a stewpan and stir till sufficiently thick; then line a flattish dish with puff paste at the bottom and edges, pour in the mixture, and bake it in a moderate oven for half an hour.

## Amber Pudding

Mix together half a pound of finely chopped suet, half a pound of bread crumbs, half a pound of sugar, a little candied peel, spice and lemon-peel, four eggs, and a pot of orange marmalade or apricot jam. Boil in a mould for three hours. For the sauce, take four ounces of butter, two ounces of sifted sugar, twelve bitter almonds pounded, and a wine-glass of brandy; beat all up to a stiff cream near the fire, and put round the pudding in the dish when served, but not a minute before, or the heat of the pudding will oil the butter!

## Madeira Pudding

Take six ounces of butter beaten to a cream, six ounces of sugar, six ounces of flour, six ounces weight of eggs in the shell. Beat the yolks and whites separately and then together; add a small wine-glassful of brandy and a little grated marmalade, (or any flavour you please). Beat well together, put it into a buttered mould, boil two hours. Serve with wine sauce.

## A Twenty Minutes Pudding

Boil one pint of new milk twenty minutes, with sugar to taste, and any flavouring you like; beat four eggs well, and mix with the milk when nearly cold. Boil all in a buttered mould for twenty minutes, and then let it stand twenty minutes, after being taken up, in the mould on the hob or oven before sending to table.

For the sauce, boil the thinly cut peel of a lemon in a little water till the flavour is extracted, rub some lumps of sugar on the lemon, to take off all the zest and add to the water in which you have boiled the lemon-peel, and make a thin syrup; add the juice of the lemon, pour round the pudding, and serve.

## Potato Pudding

Take one pound of potatoes, boiled, and beaten with a fork, a quarter of a pound of moist sugar, the juice and rind of a lemon grated, and one egg well beaten; mix thoroughly, and bake half an hour in an oven, not too quick. Serve with sweet sauce.

## Royal Pudding

Butter a plain tinned mould, and pour in the centre of it one tablespoonful of white sugar melted and let it set. Then boil a pint of cream with a piece of vanilla, add sugar to taste, and when cool strain the cream to the yolks of eight eggs well beaten. Mix thoroughly, and pour into the mould upon the hardened sugar, and set it in a stew-pan of boiling water to boil gently for half an hour. When cold, turn it out of the mould, and it will be found that the melted sugar will have coloured the outside of the pudding, and also formed a liquid brown sauce for it!

## Etiquette Note

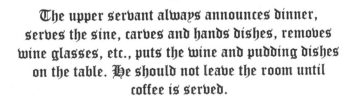

The upper servant always announces dinner, serves the wine, carves and hands dishes, removes wine glasses, etc., puts the wine and pudding dishes on the table. He should not leave the room until coffee is served.

### Recipe

*Sweet Sauce*

Melt one ounce margarine, stir in one ounce flour and mix smoothly. Add one breakfast cupful of milk gradually, and stir till it thickens. Add one teaspoon of sugar and a few drops of vanilla essence or any flavouring of your choice.

*Lemon Sauce*

Melt one ounce margarine, stir in one tablespoon flour, add half a pint of water slowly and then the juice of a lemon.

## Bakewell Pudding

Take a quarter of a pound of clarified butter, a quarter of a pound of powdered sugar, five yolks and one white of egg, and mix all well together, then add some almond flavouring to your taste. Line a dish or several small patty pans with puff paste, put a layer of raspberry or strawberry preserve on it, then put in the mixture. It requires to be well cooked in the oven before taking it out, and is generally eaten between hot and cold. Grate sugar on the top before sending to table.

## Devon Pudding

Thicken a pint of new milk with a large tablespoonful of arrowroot; beat four ounces of butter to a cream, and add four ounces of sifted sugar, four eggs, a spoonful of marmalade, and a little grated nutmeg; beat all together, and when quite light, put in a sponge cake crumbled, and mix with the milk and arrowroot, and when nearly cold bake in a dish lined with thin paste.

## Scarborough Pudding

If the apples are large sizes, take one egg for every apple. Scald and pulp the apples, then slice in half an ounce of butter, add the eggs well beaten, a little cream, candied lemon-peel, and sugar, and two tablespoonfuls of brandy. Bake in a thin paste in a moderate oven.

## A Cold Cabinet Pudding

Have ready some blancmange, and before it is stiff, put a little of it into a mould, and let it run all over it to stick to it; then ornament the mould with dried cherries and sufficient of the blancmange to make them firm, then fill up the mould with pieces of preserved apricots, a few ratafias soaked in brandy, or wine and brandy, a little citron, cut very thin, and sponge biscuits crumbled – but do not wet them too much with the brandy – and so on with cherries, or any other firm sweets, cakes, etc. till your mould is full; then fill up with the cold liquid blancmange, so as to cover all over, and let it stand all night in a cold place to set well. The cherries must be arranged to look well when turned out.

### The Berkeley Pudding

Take one pound of suet, chopped very fine, four ounces of flour, half an ounce of fine bread crumbs, three whole eggs, half a small teaspoonful of pounded mace, the same of cinnamon, a little grated nutmeg, a little grated lemon-peel, and half a pint of milk; mix all together, put into a plain mould, and boil nine hours.

For the sauce, serve a wine sauce, or as an alternative, substitute rum for the wine.

### Princess Amelia's Puddings

Take five large apples and prepare them as for sauce, and add, while hot, two ounces of butter, and when cold, two eggs thoroughly beaten, half a penny loaf grated, a little cream, nutmeg and sugar to taste; mix all together, and bake in little cups; turn them out, sift sugar over them, and serve.

## Honiton Sponge Pudding

Take three eggs, their weight in the shell in flour, butter, and sugar, and grate the rind of a lemon very fine; beat the butter to a cream, the eggs, yolks and whites separately then together; add the butter, keep on beating; then mix in the sugar, lastly the flour; then beat the whole till quite light. Put into a mould, and boil an hour and a half. Serve with lemon sauce.

## Exhibition Pudding

Take half a pound of suet, chopped very fine, a quarter of a pound of raisins, stoned, two tablespoonfuls of flour, two tablespoonfuls of sugar, the peel of a whole lemon grated, a little nutmeg and three eggs; mix together, put into a mould and boil for four hours. Serve with wine sauce.

## Wollaton Pudding

Heat a pint of new milk, and pour it upon two tablespoonfuls of flour; let it stand till cold, then add two eggs well beaten, sweeten with two tablespoonfuls of treacle, and bake. Serve immediately from the oven.

## Sir Watkin Wynn's Pudding

Take half a pound of suet, half a pound of loaf sugar, three ounces of orange marmalade, and half a pound of bread crumbs, and mix all together with three eggs and some wine or brandy.

Butter and ornament a mould with raisins, put in the ingredients, and boil for two hours and a quarter.

Serve with lemon or wine sauce.

## Etiquette Note

Be careful never to taste puddings till you are sure they are sufficiently cool, as, by disregarding this caution, you may be compelled to swallow what is dangerously hot, or be driven to the unpardonable alternative of returning it to your plate!

## Best Pancakes

Take four eggs, beat them well, and to every egg add a table-spoonful of flour; mix and beat again, then stir in gradually a pint of milk, and add a pinch of salt and a little grated nutmeg.

Have ready an omelette pan, or small round frying pan, with a little bit of butter in it on the fire; pour half a tea cupful of the batter into it, and turn round the pan (not the pancake) frequently over the fire for a minute or two, then take it off the fire, and hold it upright in front of the bars; the pancake will rise immediately and be thoroughly done. Cut the edges, sprinkle a little powdered sugar over and roll it up; and so on till you have sufficient for a dish when they must be served immediately.

## Orange Fritters

Peel three or four oranges, carefully taking off every scrap of the white part, without breaking the thin inner skin; and tear these into the natural divisions of the orange, dividing each into six or seven pieces, according to the size of the fruit; dip each piece into a light batter, fry them (not too dark) in hot fat.

Drain well, and send to table immediately, piled high on a napkin in your dish, with powdered sugar sifted over them.

## Marmalade Bread and Butter Pudding

Cut some slices of bread, without crust, a quarter of an inch in thickness, butter them well on one side, and upon this spread thickly some grated marmalade, and divide the slices into pieces about two inches long by one wide; lay these lightly in a well-buttered pudding dish; beat up three eggs with a pint of milk, and pour in upon the bread, and bake the pudding half an hour in a moderate oven.

## Friar's Omelette

Boil six large apples as for sauce, with the rind of one lemon grated, two ounces of fresh butter, and a little sugar, and when cold add two or three eggs well beaten. Take a deep dish, butter it well, strew bread crumbs thickly over the bottom and sides, put in the apples etc. and strew more bread crumbs all over the top. When baked, turn it out on to a dish, strew sugar over the top, and serve.

## Orange Pudding

Line a pudding dish with a flour and water paste ornamenting the edge also. Take six oranges – the peel of them to be pared very thin, boiled, pounded, and then rubbed through a sieve. Add the juice of the six oranges, one tea cupful of bread crumbs, six ounces of finely pounded sugar, and the yolks of four eggs; the whites should be beaten to a stiff froth, and added to the rest of the ingredients the last thing before putting in the oven. Bake three quarters of an hour in a moderate oven.

## Lemon Pudding

Take the juice of three lemons and the peel of one rubbed off with sugar, six ounces of loaf sugar pounded, and a good-sized tea cupful of bread crumbs; while these ingredients are soaking together, beat up four eggs, leaving out two whites, melt one ounce of butter, and mix all well together. Line a dish with flour and water paste, ornamenting the edge; pour in the mixture, and bake three quarters of an hour in a quick oven.

A good pudding
sharpens the wit
and softens the heart

## Baked Plum Pudding

Chop fine quarter of a pound of suet, put it into three-quarters of a pound of flour with a teaspoonful of baking powder in. Pick a quarter of a pound of plums and chop them, wash, dry, and pick a quarter of a pound of currants, two ounces of peel and two ounces of moist sugar and a pinch of mixed spice. Mix into a stiff paste with one egg beaten up in a gill or more of milk. It should be so stiff a spoon will stand up in it. Bake in a greased tin one hour.

## Rich Plum Pudding

Take one pound of jar raisins, one pound of currants, one pound of suet, chopped very fine, two ounces of almonds, blanched and pounded, and mixed in one pound of dried and sifted flour, one pound of grated bread crumbs, two ounces of citron, two ounces of orange-peel, two ounces of lemon-peel, half a nutmeg, a blade or two of mace pounded, a quarter of a pound of loaf sugar, and a pinch of salt; moisten the whole with ten beaten eggs, half a pint of cream, two glasses of wine, and a gill of brandy. Mix well together, put into a mould, and boil five hours; serve with brandy sauce. This quantity makes a large pudding.

## Christmas Pudding

Take one pound and a half of raisins, stoned, one pound and a half of currants, well washed and dried, one pound and a half of very finely chopped suet, a quarter of a pound of sugar, two ounces of citron, four large wooden spoonfuls of dried flour, four or five eggs, half a pint of milk, spice to your taste, and a glass of brandy; mix all together, and boil eight hours in a mould or basin, and serve with brandy sauce.

## Plum Duff Pudding

Mix well together, four ounces flour, two ounces bread crumbs, three ounces dripping (margarine or grated suet), two ounces sugar, half teaspoon baking powder, a little milk or one egg. Steam in basin one and a half hours. (One to two ounces dried fruit may be added, but the pudding must then be boiled for longer - two to three hours).

## Baked College Puddings

Take half a pound of grated bread, three ounces of well-washed currants, one ounce of candied peels, half an ounce of citron, two ounces of moist sugar, half a nutmeg, three eggs, and the third part of a pint of milk and pour on the bread crumbs, put in an ounce of butter, and then mix in the other ingredients. This quantity will fill six cups; bake in a moderate oven, turn the puddings out of the cups, sift pounded sugar over the tops, pour wine sauce round them, and serve.

## Buckinghamshire Pudding

Take a pint of cream, the rind of a lemon, and a bit of mace, sugar to taste, and boil together; then take out the lemon-peel, beat it in a mortar, pass it through a sieve, and put it back again to the cream; let it stand till nearly cold, then pour it gently to the yolks of six eggs, and when mixed well together put it into a mould, place the mould in a saucepan of boiling water, cover it with a lid, and set it on a slow fire to boil gently half an hour; turn it out of the mould while warm, and when it is cold pour melted currant or raspberry jelly over it, and serve.

## Lemon Surprise

Take a quarter of a pound of suet, chopped as fine as possible, half a pound of grated bread, a quarter of pound of moist sugar, the juice and finely grated rind of one lemon, and one egg; mix all well together, fill four cups, and boil half an hour; sift pounded sugar over them, and serve with lemon sauce.

## Boiled Rice Puddings

Boil a quarter of a pound of ground rice in a pint of milk and a little cream, and when almost cold add a quarter of a pound of butter, three eggs well beaten, loaf sugar to taste, and a few drops of vanilla; mix all together, pour into little cups, and boil half an hour. Serve with sweet sauce.

## Citron Pudding

Line your dish with puff paste; slice thin, orange, lemon, and citron peels, of each one ounce, six eggs (leaving out four whites) well beaten, a quarter of a pound of loaf sugar, and a quarter of a pound of butter melted; whisk all well together, and pour into the dish; bake for one hour, and serve.

## Mysterious Pudding

Beat three ounces butter to a cream; add three ounces sugar and three eggs well beaten; sift in the flour, and mix well with the jam; lastly, add one teaspoonful of baking powder. Pour into a buttered mould, which should not be full, and steam for three hours. Serve with boiled custard.

If a more economical pudding is desired, suet may be substituted for butter.

## Baked Rich Lemon Pudding

Take four eggs, a quarter of a pound of fresh butter, a gill of cream, the juice of a lemon, and flavour with lemon peel rubbed on lumps of sugar; sweeten to taste, warm the butter in the cream over the fire, and beat all well together; pour into a dish and bake. When done, cover the top with white of egg whipped to a snow froth piled up, sift over it finely pounded and sifted sugar; put it back into the oven for a few minutes, to colour the white of egg slightly, or you may brown it with a salamander.

**A salamander was a metal utensil which was heated until it was red hot, then used to brown the tops of puddings.**

## 𝕬pple 𝕮harlotte

Butter a plain tin mould; cut some slices of bread nearly a quarter of an inch thick, and cut some of these into diamonds the length of the top of your mould, cut these again across the middle to make them into three-cornered pieces, cut the rest of the slices into lengths of the height of the mould and the width of two fingers. Dip all these pieces of bread into butter melted before the fire to oil, and arrange them neatly in the mould, the three-cornered pieces at the top, each one just overlapping the other, and the same way for the lengths, standing them up round the sides of the mould.

Take one dozen good-sized apples, prepare them as for sauce, drain the water from them, and put them into a stew pan with half a pound of pounded sugar and the rind of a lemon chopped very fine; boil it for half an hour, stirring all the time, then pour it carefully into the mould which you have ready lined with the bread, and bake it for three quarters of an hour.

Turn it out of the mould, and serve immediately.

Better have some of a pudding
than none of a pie!

## Fig Pudding

Take half a pound of bread crumbs, half a pound of well chopped figs, six ounces of finely chopped suet, and six ounces of sugar, then add three eggs well beaten, a little salt, nutmeg, and cinnamon, and mix all well together; boil it in a mould four hours, and serve with wine sauce.

## Seville Pudding

Boil a small tea cupful of Carolina rice in nearly a quart of milk till soft, and the milk is nearly soaked up, then mix as much grated marmalade with it as will colour and flavour it; pour it into a well-buttered mould, and boil it again to make it turn out. Serve with wine sauce.

### Apple and Rice Soufflé

Boil some rice in milk, with a little lemon-peel and cinnamon with sugar to taste, till the milk is soaked up, and the rice soft. Fill a large tube mould with the rice, place it in a saucepan of water, and stand it in the oven for half an hour, during which time prepare some apples as for sauce, sweetening them sufficiently, and flavouring them with lemon-peel.

When the rice is done, turn it carefully out of the mould upon a dish, and fill in the hollow centre with the prepared apple; next whip the whites of three or four eggs to a stiff snow froth, pile it up high on the apples, so as to make a top to the mould of rice, sift very finely pounded sugar over it, brown it with a salamander slightly, and serve immediately.

### Arrowroot Soufflé

Take two ounces of arrowroot, two ounces of butter, a pint of milk, three ounces of sugar, a pinch of salt, and five eggs. Boil the milk with the sugar, mix the arrowroot well with a little cold milk, and then add the boiling milk gradually - stirring all the time to keep it smooth - and next the butter, then set it aside to cool. When cold, stir in the yolks of the eggs, well beaten, and some essence of vanilla, orange flower water, or any liqueur to flavour the soufflé, and lastly whip the whites of the eggs to a stiff snow froth, and whisk in with the other ingredients.

Fill a buttered soufflé mould or pudding dish, and put it into a quick oven at once; bake from half to three quarters of an hour; you will know when it is done by its rising, and the top looking set. Serve immediately, or it will fall and be good for nothing!

## Almond Soufflé

Take four ounces of blanched sweet almonds, and pound them in a mortar with two eggs till no lump can be felt, then put the almonds into a basin with four ounces of finely pounded sugar and the yolks of six eggs, and beat well for half an hour. Whip the whites of the eggs to a stiff snow froth, and then stir them with three ounces of finely pounded biscuit into the other ingredients, and put into a buttered soufflé mould and bake for half an hour, and serve immediately.

## Strawberry Soufflé

Take a large tablespoonful of flour and a quarter of a pound of butter, and simmer them over a slow fire; mix together half a pint of milk and a pot of strawberry jam, and let them boil; then rub them through a sieve, and add them to the flour and butter, with a little sugar to sweeten if needed. Put in the yolks of five eggs, beat up the whites of the eggs to snow, and stir them gently into other ingredients; put into a plain mould, and boil an hour. Serve it with wine sauce in which you have put a little of the strawberry jam rubbed through a sieve. Raspberry jam may also be used for this soufflé instead of strawberry.

## Apricot Pudding

Stew six large apricots with some sugar till quite tender, break them up and when cold add the yolks of six eggs and then the whites of two well beaten; mix well together with a pint of good cream, and more sugar if required. Line your dish with puff paste, and pour in the ingredients; bake half an hour in a moderate oven, strew sifted sugar over it, and serve.

## Etiquette Note

Servants'rules for waiting at table:
move quickly but quietly
do not speak unless it is absolutely necessary
do not rattle forks, spoons, dishes etc
do not breathe heavily.

# Fruit Pie

Pie-crust is made either short or flaky according to the way the fat, whether it be butter, lard, suet, or dripping, is put into the flour. For short crust, it is rubbed into the flour before the flour is wetted; for flaky, it is rolled in afterwards.

Take half a pound of flour, mix with it half a teaspoonful of baking powder, and rub lightly into a quarter of a pound of butter. Wet it with sufficient cold water to make a stiff paste; the quantity required depends on the quality of the flour. Roll it out two inches larger than the pie dish to cover, fill the dish with fruit, put four tablespoonfuls of moist sugar to a quart of fruit. For dry fruit, as apples, and plums, and green gooseberries, put in half a gill of water; juicy fruit requires none. Sprinkle a little sugar over, and bake half an hour in a moderate oven.

# Marrow Pudding

Skin and cut up the marrow. Mix three tablespoons wheatmeal flour with one pint milk and stir three ounces sugar, one teaspoon ground ginger, one egg into it. Pour into pie dish. Cover with pastry. Bake half hour.

## Melrose Pudding

Mix quarter pound flour, quarter pound bread crumbs, three ounces suet, one teacup jam, one teacup milk, half tablespoon sugar, half teaspoon bicarbonate soda, one egg well beaten and lastly add half teaspoon vinegar. Boil in a greased basin covered with greased paper for two to three hours.

## Baked Custard

To the yolks of four eggs beaten lightly with a little sugar pour one pint of boiling milk, flavour to taste, line a dish with a little piece of pie-crust, pour in the custard, and bake three-quarters of an hour. A common one can be made of two whole eggs.

## Bread Pudding

Soak half a pound of pieces of bread in cold water, any crusts however stale will do, provided they are not mouldy. Squeeze them dry, and pour on them one quart of boiling milk. Cover, and let them swell. Beat up two eggs with two ounces of sugar, stir into the pudding, put in a quarter of a pound of plums or currants. Bake in a greased dish half an hour or boil in a buttered basin for two hours.

## Batter and Black Cap Puddings

Eight ounces of flour, half a teaspoonful of baking powder, two eggs, a pint of milk. Mix the flour with the baking powder and a pinch of salt. Break the eggs into a cup, beat them lightly with a little of the milk, mix them by degrees quite smoothly into the flour so that there are no lumps, then add the rest of the milk. Grease a basin, pour the pudding in through a strainer, flour the cloth thickly after dipping it in boiling water, tie it securely, and boil gently for an hour and a half. Black cap pudding is made by throwing in a quarter of a pound of currants after the batter is in the basin.

## Castle Puddings

Take two eggs in the shells, and the weight of them in sugar and also in flour, and three ounces of butter. Put the butter into a basin, and set it by the fire till half melted, then beat it to a cream. Beat the eggs ten minutes, mix them gently with the butter, then add the sugar, flour, a pinch of pounded cinnamon, a tablespoonful of orange-flower water, and mix thoroughly. Pour the mixture into six small buttered cups, bake and then turn out and serve with a sauce of your fancy.

## Bachelor's Pudding

Pare, core, and chop two apples finely; add four ounces of currants, bread crumbs and two ounces sugar; beat three eggs, add lemon peel and juice, then mix all well together and put in a buttered basin. Tie a cloth over this, and boil three hours.

## Aunt Margaret's Pudding

Rub two ounces of lard or butter into the flour, mix well together; mix into crumbs with egg, two tablespoonfuls of sugar, quarter of a pound of flour, half a teaspoonful of baking powder. Butter a mould and put in a layer of ingredients and a layer of jam. Steam two hours, and serve with your favourite family sauce!

## Betsy Pudding

Mix all together half of a pound flour, quarter of a pound of suet, one teaspoonful baking powder, small tea cupful jam or treacle, one egg, enough milk to make a stiff batter. Steam for not less than two hours. Serve with sweet sauce.

## Rainbow Pudding

Cream four ounces of butter and four ounces of sugar; add eggs, five ounces of flour, half teaspoonful of baking powder and a little milk. Divide into five basins, and use the following colourings: cochineal, brown (using chocolate powder), heliotrope and green; put in alternative spoonfuls in a buttered mould and steam one and a half hours.

## Etiquette Note

**For dessert, a fresh plate knife and fork, doyley and finger bowl should be provided for each person**

## London Pudding

Line a pie-dish with good puff-paste; put a good layer of apricot jam at the bottom of the dish, then some sponge cakes on top of jam; then make the following mixture:- Mix one tablespoonful of flour with a piece of butter, and sweeten it well; hot quarter of a pint of milk; pour over the flour and boil. When boiled, mix in the yolks of three eggs, pour it over the sponge cakes and bake; whisk the whites of egg to a stiff froth, spread on the top, and put in the oven to set.

## Alexander Pudding

Line a pie-dish with puff-paste, and cover the bottom with stewed apples, or any kind of jam. Mix three large spoons of stale bread crumbs with the same quantity of caster sugar, and juice of one lemon, with the rind grated; mix well all together, and add a tea cupful of milk and two well-beaten eggs. When all have been well-beaten together, pour it into the dish over the apple, and bake for about half an hour in a moderate oven.

## Pineapple Pudding

Arrange pineapple pieces in a pie-dish; mix the yolks of two eggs with two ounces of sugar and pineapple juice; melt two ounces butter in a pan and add two ounces flour gradually; then the milk; let boil for three minutes, stirring all the time; add sugar, juice, eggs; and as soon as it thickens, pour over pineapple. Put the pudding in the oven to heat through, and then leave to cool; beat up the whites of eggs stiffly and cover top of pudding with them.

### Patriotic Pudding

Take two ounces of lard and butter mixed, and two tablespoonfuls of white sugar, beat to a cream; add one egg well-beaten, then stir in three tablespoonfuls of flour, one of ground rice, a small teaspoonful of baking powder, and enough milk to make a batter that will just pour.

Put into a buttered basin, steam one hour and serve with sweet sauce.

### Newark Pudding

Beat the yolks of two eggs, add half a cup of bread crumbs soaked in half-pint of milk; stir to a smooth batter; add one tablespoonful of ground rice, (wet first with a little cold milk); add the rest of the milk, butter, raisins, and a tablespoonful of sugar; lastly, the whites well whisked. Put in a buttered dish and bake one hour; turn out, and serve with sweet sauce.

### Leicester Pudding

Rub quarter pound butter into half pound flour and one teaspoon baking powder. Mix to a batter with one egg and one teacup milk.; beat well. Put jam at bottom of greased basin, pour in the batter and steam one and half hours.

## Canary Pudding

Melt three ounces of butter, add three ounces sugar and finely-minced lemon peel; gradually dredge in three ounces of flour, keep the mixture well stirred; whisk the three eggs and add to the pudding; blend thoroughly, put in a buttered basin, boil two hours.

## Marmalade Pudding

Place in a basin - quarter pound of suet (finely chopped), quarter pound bread crumbs, quarter pound marmalade, add quarter pound of sugar; mix well together. Beat eggs to a froth, and gradually mix with the other ingredients; put in a buttered mould. Tie down with floured cloth and boil for two hours, turn out and strew fine sifted sugar over the top. This pudding will look very pretty if stoned raisins are tastefully arranged before the mixture is poured in.

## Feather Pudding

Put jam or treacle at bottom of greased basin, mix one breakfast cupful flour, one dessert spoonful margarine, three ounces sugar, half teaspoon bicarbonate of soda, half teaspoon cream of tartar, one beaten egg, one teacup milk, add to basin and boil for two hours.

## 'Kiss Me Quick' Pudding

Mix one breakfast cupful flour, one teacup fine sugar, one ounce butter (rubbed in), one egg, half teaspoonful ginger, one small teaspoonful carbonate of soda, two tablespoonfuls of jam, half tea cupful milk and a pinch of salt.

Steam the above for three hours and serve with sauce.

### Kissing don't last - cooking do!
George Meredith 1828-1909

## Banana Rolls

Rub two ounces butter into quarter pound of flour, add salt and yolk of one egg. Mix with a little water, and knead into a firm paste; roll out as thinly as possible, and cut into oblong shapes. Remove skin and split bananas lengthwise; spread each half with preserve (raspberry preferred) and lay the halves together again. Cover with pastry, and bake in a moderate oven.

## Ginger Pudding

Dissolve one teaspoon bicarbonate soda in one teacup milk and add to half pound flour, three ounces suet or butter chopped finely, one ounce sugar, one ounce lemon peel (candied), two tablespoons treacle, one teaspoon ginger and mix well. Put in greased basin. Cover with greased paper and boil two to three hours.

## Jubilee Pudding

Make one pint of jelly, allow it to cool, then pour over four sponge cakes placed in a glass dish. When set, pour either thick cream or custard over it.

As is the cook
So is the kitchen

## Imperial Pudding

Put four ounces flour in a dish, rub in lightly one ounce butter and one and a half ounces lard, add two ounces sugar and pinch of salt, then one egg and three tablespoonfuls of milk well-beaten; mix well together, then add half a tablespoonful baking powder. Grease a basin, put a good layer of jam at the bottom, then add the pudding. Put a greased paper on the top, and steam for one hour. Serve with sweet sauce.

## Perfect Prune Pudding

Soak half a pound stoned prunes overnight. Cook them with one apple (peeled and sliced finely) till tender (about one hour). Put them into greased pie dish. Add sugar, or golden syrup, to taste. Make a stiff batter with one and a half teacups flour, one teaspoon baking powder, pinch of salt, one egg, well beaten and one and half teacups milk. Spread the batter over the fruit and bake three quarters hour in a moderate oven.

## My Pet Pudding

Sweeten one pint milk and flavour with vanilla. Boil it, then pour over quarter of pound of bread crumbs and leave to soak, then add the well-beaten yolks of two eggs. Spread a pie-dish with apricot jam and pour in the mixture; bake for half-hour, then smother the top with a snow made of the whites of eggs well-beaten with some icing sugar added. Put the pudding in the oven until lightly brown.

## Etiquette Note

Setting the sideboard is a duty which few, except the most experienced servants understand. It should first be covered with a cloth; some spoons, forks knives, wine, finger-bowls, clean wine glasses and dishes for pudding should be neatly arranged.
Until the servant knows his work thoroughly, the mistress should inspect the table and sideboard carefully.

𝕳appiness is -
𝕬 good bank account,
𝕬 good cook - and
𝕬 good digestion.

## Victoria Pudding

Two eggs, their weight in flour, butter and sugar, two teaspoonfuls baking powder, jam, a little vanilla flavour. Beat the butter and sugar well together, add the eggs and vanilla, beat well and add the flour. Grease a basin and cover the bottom with jam, put in the mixture, and steam one and a half hours.

## Albert Pudding

The weight of two eggs in sugar, butter, and flour, some sultanas or raisins, a good flavouring of lemon juice, and a pinch of salt. Cream the butter and sugar together, add one egg at a time, and part of the flour sifted in; well mix it, then at the last add the sultanas. Steam in well-greased cups for half an hour, or, if put into one mould, one hour. Serve with sweet sauce on the dish.

### A Novel Pudding

Take three of four large apples, peel, core, slice, an
put into pie-dish, adding two ounces of sugar, piece c
butter the size of a walnut, and a few cloves. Cover thickl
with bread-crumbs to form crust. Bake in a moderate ove:
for three-quarters of an hour. Serve with cream.

### Manchester Pudding

Boil one pint new milk, add three ounces brea(
crumbs, grated rind of a lemon, three eggs, three ounce
butter melted, sweeten to taste. Line a dish with puff-paste
cover the bottom with jam and add milk mixture. Bake

### Brighton Pudding

Mix together with a little milk into a smooth paste, on(
cupful flour, one cupful suet, a pinch of salt, half cupfu
sugar, one egg, one teaspoonful baking powder. Put abou
three tablespoonfuls of treacle or jam at the bottom of :
basin, pour mixture over, and steam for about two to thre(
hours. Currants or raisins could be used if preferred.

## Cabinet Pudding

Take half a pound of bread crumbs scalded in milk, to which add a cup of cream, three eggs well beaten, a little flour, and a very little nutmeg. Have mould well buttered and stuck with raisins, pour the mixture in, and boil for two hours. Serve with sweet sauce.

## Thornton Pudding

Two eggs, their weight in flour and butter, the weight of one in sugar, one teaspoonful baking powder, two tablespoonfuls of strawberry jam at the bottom of a basin. Boil two and a half hours.

## Economical Fritters

Cut three or four slices of stale bread into three or four pieces. Mix one tablespoon flour and one teacup milk to a smooth batter and soak bread in it for half an hour. Melt a little fat in deep frying pan and, when boiling, drop the bread in and fry until golden brown (four to five minutes). Drain on paper. Spread half the pieces with jam and put the other pieces on top. Sprinkle a little sugar on each and serve hot.

## Chocolate Sponge

Pour one pint boiling milk on three ounces chocolate.
Cover basin with lid or plate till the chocolate dissolves.
Then add half teacup hot water, three ounces sugar and
beaten yolk of one egg. Cook mixture gently till it
thickens, stirring constantly but not allowing it to boil.
When thick, take saucepan off. Beat till it begins to set.
Then whisk in the white of egg (previously stiffly beaten).
Whip well and turn into wet mould. A pinch of salt or
juice or half a lemon improves the flavour.

## Coronation Pudding

Rub lard into half pound flour, add quarter pound of
sugar, grated rind and juice of lemon, baking powder, two
eggs and one tea cupful milk, and beat well together. Well
grease a pudding basin, and put two tablespoonfuls of
treacle in the bottom, pour in the mixture, and steam two
hours. Serve with lemon sauce.

## Date Pudding

Mix quarter pound stoned dates, quarter pound of suet
and quarter pound flour with a little milk and steam four
hours.

## Crimson Shape

Boil one and a half pounds red fruit (raspberries, blackberries, damsons etc) with water and three ounces sugar till there are one and a half pints of juice. Put through a sieve. Mix four dessert spoonfuls of cornflour and three ounces sugar with a little cold water and stir into liquid when boiling. Boil five to ten minutes.

Turn into a wet mould and serve cold.

## Etiquette Note

When eating, avoid every kind of audible testimony to the fact and never speak while you have anything in your mouth.

### Eastbourne Pudding

Rub two ounces margarine into flour. Add two ounces sultanas, one ounce sugar, one teaspoon baking powder. Mix well with egg and milk. Bake in greased pie-dish for thirty to forty minutes.

### Brown Betty Pudding

Fill a greased pie-dish with alternate layers of six apples, cored and sliced, two breakfast cups brown bread crumbs and three ounces stoned raisins, also adding one tablespoon sugar and half teaspoon mixed spice. Mix the syrup with the warm water and pour over the pudding. Cover with bread crumbs and bake one hour in good oven.

### Lemon Sago Pudding

Wash one teacup sago and simmer in four teacups water till quite clear. Add three tablespoons treacle, one teacup sugar, the juice and rinds of two lemons. Boil for five minutes, stirring. Pour into a mould, previously rinsed with cold water. Serve cold with custard.

The proof of the pudding
Is in the eating

Old English Proverb

## Prune Snowball

Line a greased basin with half pound unpolished rice (boiled). Pour in the prunes. Place a layer of rice on top. Cover with greased paper and steam one hour. Turn out and serve with sweet sauce.

## Preserved Ginger Pudding

Cream quarter pound margarine with two ounces sugar. Beat in one egg and one teacup milk. Add quarter pound flour, half teaspoon bicarbonate soda, one table-spoon preserved ginger, chopped. Quickly pour into a greased basin. Cover with greased paper. Boil for one and a half to two hours. Serve with sweet sauce into which one tablespoon of liquor from the ginger jar should be stirred before removing from the fire.

## Semolina Cheesecake

Boil half pint milk and one lemon rind. Remove the latter and stir in the semolina. Cook till thick (five to ten minutes). Add one tablespoon currants, juice of the lemon and one egg, beaten. When cold, put on pastry, previously placed on patty pans, or on one dish. Bake twenty minutes.

### Fruit in Batter Pudding

Half fill a greased pie-dish with apples, finely sliced (gooseberries, rhubarb, currants, plums, or any other fresh fruit). Mix together two large tablespoons flour, one teaspoon baking powder and one dessertspoon of sugar. Add one and a half pints of milk to one egg and stir into the mixture. Pour over the fruit. Bake in moderate oven for one and a quarter hours.

### Semolina Pudding

Boil half pint milk and half pint water. Drop in two ounces semolina. Add two ounces coconut meal, one teaspoon sugar, half teaspoon cinnamon. Stir till in thickens (about five minutes). Pour into greased pie dish. Bake twenty to thirty minutes.

Alternatively, pour into greased pudding basin, cover with greased paper and boil one hour. Turn out and serve with jam.

## Half Pay Pudding

Mix well together, quarter pound flour, quarter pound dripping, quarter pound bread crumbs, quarter pound raisins, quarter pound currants, one ounce candied peel, two tablespoons treacle, one teaspoon baking powder, half pint milk. Placed in greased basin, cover with greased paper and boil two to three hours.

## Summer Pudding

Line a greased basin with the bread. Pour in one and half pound stewed fresh fruit, filling the basin quite full. Cover the top with one round or slices of bread. Put a weighted plate on top. Turn out carefully when cold. Can be served with custard.

## Syrup Tart

Roll out pastry thinly. Cut size of plate. Put band of pasty all round and mark edges with knife or scissors. Put on it one warmed teacup golden syrup and four table-spoons brown bread crumbs about two inches thick. Bake twenty minutes in hot oven.

## Baked Chocolate Pudding

Boil one pint milk and add two ounces chocolate powder, three ounces brown bread-crumbs and two ounces sugar. Cool for a little. Add the beaten yolks from two eggs. Whip whites and place on top. Bake in greased pie-dish fifteen minutes.

*The Etiquette Collection is a series of pocket-sized books full of social secrets and hints for correct conduct. Collect the set!*

### THE ETIQUETTE OF AN ENGLISH TEA
How to serve a perfect English afternoon tea;
tea traditions, superstitions, recipes - including
how to read your fortune in the
tea-leaves afterwards.

### ETIQUETTE FOR COFFEE LOVERS
Coffee the way it ought to be!
Coffee lovers will enjoy this look at the history
of coffee drinking, its secrets, recipes, hints
and coffee chat. The perfect companion
for those who enjoy coffee time.

### THE ETIQUETTE OF POLITENESS
Good sense and good manners.
How to be polite and well-bred at all times.

### THE ETIQUETTE OF LOVE AND COURTSHIP
A guide for romantics.
Flirting, temptation, first impressions:
essential advice for lovers.

*Copper Beech Gift Books
are designed and printed
in Great Britain.*